A PAINTING ON THE NIGHT

EDWARD G. SCHENKEL

A Painting On The Night
Copyright © 2020 by Edward G. Schenkel

ISBN: 978-9083056104

Instagram: @edwardschenkelpoet

Cover design by Edward G. Schenkel

For my wife and son

CONTENTS

LET US DANCE

Let us dance
In the Japanese garden
Where seasons don't matter
And time doesn't fly

Just the smile of a flower
Granting eternal power
To the moon and the stars
And the magic of night

A PAINTING ON THE NIGHT

The fires of the past
Have been burning up my mind
My skin's been marked with scars
That I need to leave behind

But now an angel with white gloves
Sparks some light upon my life
And that fire lit with love
Draws a painting on the night

UNBROKEN CORDS

There's so much about you
That keeps me dancing around you
Trapped in the crossfire
One truthful liar
Of unspoken words

When I'm around you
I feel I'm nothing without you
But a mad fool on a wire
About to set fire
To unbroken cords

BOSPORUS SWEET

I gaze across my Bosporus sweet
Its mighty beauty still the same
The oriental breeze calms down my heat
As it carries the whispers of your name

I vision my love on the other side
My heart is pounding between its beats
And I go stumbling 'cross the bridge
Like opening doors of rooms en suite

I recall how you welcomed me before
Let my weary head rest on your chest
Made me miss you - come back for more
I'm in your hands but I feel blessed

Across the water, on your side
My shaky hands knock on your door
But when it opens, it turns the tide
And I'm not going back - no more

CAPTAIN

The guys in the field
Trapped behind the brick wall
So frightened to yield
And afraid to get called

But the strong - and so the weak -
On your command, on your call
Will jump into the deep
For their captain, for all

CANDLE BLOWN

Blow the candle
Smell the smoke
Smell and watch it dance
Watch it twirl
Watch it dissolve
The night into
The night

SHADES OF PINK

My mind is tossing shades of pink
Flickering frames of our first date
And I gaze at the dishes in the sink
But can't recall I did that plate

The sky's been painting shades of pink
A tone unknown to angels yet
On homey grounds, for us, I think
But I would observe it in Tibet

I'm writing in seven grades of pink
With shaky hands across my heart
Engraving us in indelible ink
So that our love will never part

I'm seeing seven shades of pink
And on the brink of virgin snow in May
I look at it without a blink
And your heart is coming down my way

BUDDY

23

Regardless the times
I've been struggling nights
To beat the darkness inside
In my rumbles, my fights

You've been the sparkle inside
That clean cuddling light
That keeps my passion on fire
My buddy, my life

ROOM WITH A VIEW

25

My weekend mistress
My concealed rendezvous
My back-stage princess
My inconvenient truth

My sweetest incense
My blooming taboo
My play-mate suspense
My room with a view

HEADFIRST

I've been living like a fool
Digging out for jewels
But now the sinner's ill chanting
Keeps my spirit advancing
To get my life reimbursed

I truly found my cure
In living by new rules
Where the fiddlers are jamming
And the ripples are dancing
As I dive in headfirst

THE PLACE WE CALL OUR HOME

When my heart beats like a battering bass
And my mind cooks like a pressure dome
I think of you, my king and ace
And I feel like I'm back home

It may take ages before I see your face
And there sure are times I feel alone
But then I call you just in case
And I feel that I am home

When my life is on a chilling pace
My room turns to a whispering dome
I dream of you and our first base
And I hush that you're my home

We may be miles away from full embrace
And we can't share a brush or comb
But our hearts still share that same old place
The place we call our home

CHRISTMAS IN AUTUMN

The birds tag along - the thinning trees
Their whistles merely forgotten

But the words of their songs - they spring in me
Aware of Christmas in autumn

MY LOVE

A bond, for sure, a bond,
Is what you have with me

A friend, of course, a friend
Is what you mean to me

A love, indeed, a love,
Is what this is to me

My love, oh yes, my love,
Is what you are to me

THE SHADOWS

The painting in the moonlit night
Seals the memory of your stolen smile
A true mirror for my soul
You're my silver, you're my gold
You're the treasure of my life

I frame your spirit in mine
Feel your energy in the lonely night
Murky figures where I go
So much clearer though - the shadows
That your footsteps left behind

LET YOUR MIND JUMP

Keep your spirit up
Hold your head up high
Let your mind jump
Into the infinite sky

RAIN

I sing for you with pride
About the story of our fight
How much I shared your pain
Withstood the pouring rain
And sealed the teardrops in my heart

Now I sing for you with pride
About the glory in my life
I hear you humming the refrain
All through the buzzing rain
And feel your cheers throbbing my heart

EDWARD G. SCHENKEL

CAFÉ AU SOURIRE

41

I'm reading the menu
In an urban café

Coffee of all kinds
A hundred variations
But I cannot choose
They're not familiar
They're not like home

So, I just order some black
While I think of you
And your café au sourire
Awaiting the cup
Awaiting your smile

WHATEVER FUTURE BRINGS

Life proposes a chance to fight
I feel the breeze of the passing train
Eyes closed witness a glance of light
A new nightmare passed in vain

Years of ruined self esteem
My soul held back by expectations
When fear ruled the best of dreams
Controlled and cracked by intimidation

Schemes burning down the tones
Lonely twirls of unknown chords
Your dreams I've turned into my own
This trophy girl wins her own awards

Your dreams I've turned into my own
I've shaken the burden of your past
I will flourish as the flower I've grown
Whatever future brings, will last

WITHOUT YOU

45

Dreams filming
The face that is mine

Blood pumping
In opposite circles

Words melting
On the heat of my tongue

Tears filling
The flooded well inside

Love's killing
My life without you

STRINGS OF LOVE

When I watch you swing
High above the playground
And I see your smile
Swinging to the clouds

Then I start to sing
My words - without a sound
As I see in your eyes
The strings of love - out of bounds

GUIDE A LA CARTE

Behold this magic stone
Keep it flowing in your hands
Treasure it dearly
And when pressure is fiercely
I reside in your heart

So when tragic alone
It knows and understands
And it will answer sincerely
All questions within thee
It guides a la carte

GOODBYE STRANGER!

I stretch my hand out upwards
And see you do the same
Our flat hands touch each other
I don't even know your name

The sound of silence we embrace
Gone the chatter from the flight
Just the smile that cracks your face
Before we drop our hands – goodbye!

NO EYES TO SEE

No hours in the day
No more days in the year
No drops in the rain
And no breath in the air

No leaves on the trees
No more sun left to shine
No naked eye to see
And no reflection of mine

CARRY ON

Carry on
With your endeavours

Be smart, be bold
Be everything you want

And I will watch
Your heart grow

In silence
From a distance

I will be there
With guidance

I will always be ready
For your call

MAIN STAGE

Each time you light your magic match
Cupid's sparks start jumping 'round
They conquer my heart in just a snatch
And toss it nowhere to be found

The umbrella of Havana nights
Brings passion to the basement floor
The deceptive darkness of the light
Lifts us up for ten times more

Fresh morn' sunlight leaves a shiver
As dawn closes in from every side
Love's still rowing up Tequila River
In a desperate effort to beat the tide

But just as riversides reach breaking point
My lullaby flies from your prison cage
'Cos whether concert hall or downtown joint
I need to sing my song on a main stage

LOVE'S FACES

Love's first call at dawn
Joys about this day
We meet

Lovebirds in our hands
Sing aloud and embrace
The heat

Love stirs all it can
Holds doubts in our face
Of cheat

Love's third final chance
Brings clouds to my place
In defeat

Love's words in the sand
Fade out by the waves
In retreat

THE SONG OF MY LIFE

I rattle and hum
Until the sinner lifts the curtain
I'm a fighter awaiting
The twilight engaging
So strong that I thrive

The battle may be long
But the winner is certain
I'm a writer creating
Till the spotlights embrace
The song of my life

62

EDWARD G. SCHENKEL

MY SPECIAL FRIEND

63

I got you no watch
Or fancy gift
To impress your eyes
With dollar bills

I got you no candy
Or silly pills
To sweeten your mouth
With honeyed slick

I just got some words
For you, from me
That I wish you well
And the best in life

I just got some words
For you, from me
That I'll be your friend
'till the end of time

NEW BEGINNING

65

In the cold of the night
The fun lights are dimming
And the red ball decides
On all new beginnings

I'm folding all my lies
Let the sun rise within me
And shine some of its light
On troubled mysteries

LIGHT UPON MY SHADOWS

67

Let the streets turn into channels
Filled by building's waterfalls
Turn the street lights into candles
In a million restaurants

Hear the songs on the piano
Sounds of kindness a la carte
Spread some light upon my shadows
And the brightness of my heart

EDWARD G. SCHENKEL

ONE MORE DANCE

The wind jamming through the streets
Searching for your auburn hair
Let it dance upon its beats

One more time
Just one more time
Before it leaves

Raindrops sliding down my cheeks
Merging with my humble prayers
Hear them drop and start the beat

One more dance
Just one more dance
Upon my feet

BE PATIENT

Be gracious
And nice
Be courageous
My child

But above all
Be patient
This time

Dawn will come by
To cover the night

MEMORIES ON CARBON PAPER

The lights on my deck feel homey
But they're blurring the spotlights on you
I'm tired of my memory roaming
In search of some kind of truth

We must have had some history
I can see it in the pictures of us too
It's just a doggone mystery
That I can't remember losing you

Each night in my dreams
Stars a beautiful girl in the garden of Eden
But when the morning light appears
Our pas de deux twirls start receding

I can feel she was my treasury
But I have been trying so hard to name her
So let me reclaim just one memory
And write it down on carbon paper

74

SABII FALLS

75

I gather your wishes
To blend with my tears
Before I spread my wings
One last time

And I make all this love
Plunge onto the world
My Sabii Falls forever
In the corner of your hearts

EDWARD G. SCHENKEL

TWO ADULTS, ONE CHILD

Here we are
Three steps above the ground
The world rocking
And rolling
Under our bare feet

On a farm
With a straw in our mouth
The universe hides
Two adults, one child
Under an apple tree

SPRING IS COMING

Icy rivers cutting through my cheeks
They wake me before the silent night
It feels like I have slept for weeks
With cheating dreams in broad daylight

Sugary words from a bittersweet tongue
That once tossed jitters through my veins
I lost my guard when I heard your song
You'd fake me sunshine when it rains

Now I watch the pond down at the park
Its gloomy glance just comforts me
The ducklings in silence after dark
No quacking lies nor hollow plea

I've been a rainbow all along
Despite of all your crap I hear
Your words get misty in the sun
And spring is coming near and near

THE LION'S HEART

81

One should never doubt
The cry of a lion's heart
As it gently weeps
And never sleeps
In the face of the night

Only a fool would doubt
The might of the lion's heart
It may intensely bleed
But it transgresses the heat
As it engages the fight

THAT ONE FACE

A new moon has passed
As the mystery awakes
And drum beats adjust
The daylight tune breaks

And a new face surpasses
All those pictured on screen
But it needs special glasses
To disclose the unseen

It's hard to find rhymes
In books of restless hearts
Or read between the lines
As they crook the fine arts

So many faces appear
Dark night and bright day
But by now it's still unclear
What face is meant to stay

No matter what mock dish
Is presented at morn' start
The thing that really rocks is
That one face to your heart

LAUNCH ME TO YOUR STAR

Sweet little bumblebee
Come and feel the pride in me
Of how you put up a fight
Fought your battles like a knight
And conquered all our hearts

Sweet little tumblebee
Shine your healing light on me
The cure for all dark nights
'Cos with that purest light
You launch me to your star

86

BURNING CAGE

I thought I showed you well before
In many subtle ways
That I've loved you friends and more
In past and present days

But now the times are changing
Warm memories been turning older
And the few times we're engaging
Your chilly eyes have grown yet colder

I still feel the straight up fire
Inside it's like a burning cage
And to miss you - flames get higher
Thrive my heart towards a rage

In your face I might confess
That it's ok to be apart
I know my love should be less
But I can't ban you from my heart

THE PART I LOVE

Your face, your lips,
your heart and soul
your eyes, your hips,
your love, your all

BLACK BUTTERFLIES

Release the butterflies
In the dawning light
The black wings
Wet and heavy

Their steady strokes
Whispering
Like a brush
On virgin white canvas

Paint the picture
Of heavenly angels
Holding hands
With the new-born void

92

THE RISE OF THE MORNING SUN

93

Run with me and lay down
Where the crawling fog
Touches down on the sand
Soft and wet
And let's enjoy
The rise
Of the morning sun

DAD

Lay your head here on my chest
Just like you used to do before
When times were at their best
Like when we wrestled on the floor

Just watching the tube at home
Or on those summer camping trips
Where we often watched the stars
And grab each other's chips

Now the car's lacking its driver's seat
And the ship's missing its steering wheel
No crowd cheering, when we compete
The court must do without appeal

She's out there in the air somewhere
And she's in them drops of rain
With each breath we swallow part of her
And feel her hug flow through our veins

But whenever she will take a nap
Just know I'll be around for you
And whenever you think I'm crap
Just know I miss your mommy too

SNOW

When snowflakes
Touch the mountain's sides
And rest upon its slopes

It's like the

Silky wedding dress
Sliding on the graceful bride
Ready to be shown

DANCING ON THE STILL OF NIGHT

The folded cards
Now open wide
Our stories told
By words inside

They seem so still
On paper white
Yet they dance
Within my mind

My dearest moments
Of you and I
In scribbled words
With love implied

Whenever I need
They come to life
And then we dance
On the still of night

SPECTRUM OF MY HEART

It is irrelevant
If you have autism
Or Asperger's
Or no diagnosis at all
As long as
You're within the spectrum
Of my heart

LET SNOW BURN

One more run
Just one more turn
On cutting edge
Let snow burn

THE NIGHT'S BEEN LACKING STARS

The night's been lacking stars
But I can smell the morning beauty
Of the sea and the washed-out shells
And so the flowers, as they shower
In the field of life

My mind's been trapped inside the dark
But the fresh air comes to soothe me
Comfort me and my squashed-out self
As I recharge my power, four minutes an hour
And feed the light

MY BUTTERFLY

When I laugh
In the middle of the night
I laugh with you
Tears running through
Your giggling eyes

When I dance
To the rhythm of the night
I dance with you
A dance for two
In the twinkling lights

When I sing
In the still of the night
I sing with you
Our sweetest tunes
Until the dawning light

And when I fly
Beyond the morning light
I'll fly for you
Spread my wings for you
My butterfly

PUPPY EYES

When I look
Into your puppy eyes
It's hard to imagine
That you're the true defender
Of a lion's heart

WHEN MORNING BLOWS ITS WHISTLE

When morning blows its whistle
And the sun sets fire to the night
See the dawning dew as crystals
Reflect the lightning light of life

Let me embark onto this mission
Burn the pyre where I hide
Let me board and grow my vision
Collect the lightning light inside

LEAVES IN MY MIND

113

I can't think clear
My thoughts are a mess
All things I must do
And things to confess

Inside of my head
Grow trees of all kinds
While the wind - from all sides
Blows leaves through my mind

YOU ARE LOVED

Your smile's like a flower
That colours my life
Your smile grants the power
To put up my fights

And that sun in your smile
Comes to shine down on me
It reflects in my eyes
You are loved, just like me

SO BLACK THE ROSES

So black the roses
So dark the night
I need you more
Than I ever might

SHADOW DANCING

The pianos singing to the beat
Of the rolling thunder through the sky
Shadows playing hide and seek
In search of the colors of the night

I just enjoy myself in silence
Watch this brittle work of art
The gracious grooves of your dance
To the rhythm of my heart

REBORN

Entrust your reborn heart
To the phoenix of the night
Let it rise from the horizon
Let it shine upon your flight

#BFF

I will be anything for you, my friend,
A gentle breeze that tickles the rose in your hair
A joyful mate when the times are fun
A tutorial guide in the walk of life

I will be anything for you, my girl,
A comforting shoulder when red becomes blue
A patient ear when there's no one there
To calm your young and restless heart

And I will not ask for anything back, from you
My joy's the passion of your heart
And I will not ask for anything back, from you
But that smile you gave me at the start

JUDGMENT DAY

My spirit bright
All prayers done
Awaiting the light
And the whispered songs

The scars of night
Blur the shade
And my star shines bright
On judgment day

THANK YOU

For the guidance you provide
With the whispers off your tongue
For the silence brought to life
In the whistles of your songs

For the melodies you sing
That grow flowers in the sand
For the remedies you bring
That empower every man

For the candles that you blow
With wishes of delight
For the courage that you show
And the spirits you enlight

For the heroic fights you win
Inspiring glowing works of art
For the poetic rhymes you spin
Thin lines sewn across my heart

ABOUT THE AUTHOR

It was not very likely for Edward G. Schenkel to publish a poetry collection. Being an uber nerd in high school and far beyond, a career in software and technology seemed the more natural path to follow. Years later, after meeting his wife, he started writing small pieces eventually turning more and more into poems. It was also his wife who convinced him to publish, at all.

The author holds a MSc degree in Informatics. When not writing, he enjoys to run, watch movies & sports and to drink loads of coffee. He currently lives in Schagen, The Netherlands.

A Painting On The Night is the author's debut poetry collection.